Contents

About the writers

Erica Roberts is a former paediatric oncologist. As an Anglican priest, she is passionate about her role as city chaplain for older people in Southampton. Supporting this work, she founded the charity Caraway and is delighted to be part of the BRF Anna Chaplaincy network. She loves being creative in worship and engaging those who live with dementia. In her free time, you'll find her walking along a deserted beach with her Westie.

John Rackley has over 40 years' experience in pastoral ministry. He is an associate minister with a Leicestershire LEP and Methodist Circuit. He is currently researching the relationship between biography and belief.

Derek Morgan is a recently retired IT professional, having spent over 30 years in software development roles. From his 40-plus years as a Christian, he knows his gifting will never be as a preacher or evangelist, but his God-given passion is facilitating those who are! You will always find him somewhere in church using his gifts in technical, practical, musical and IT activities. He lives on the south coast of England.

Clare O'Driscoll worked in Bible translation administration for 13 years, before leaving for a more freelance, child-friendly set-up. Since then, she's been giving Spanish and French tuition, writing articles for Christian publications and providing press support for a local youth charity. She is also on the team of volunteer editors at *Magnet* magazine. She lives in West Sussex with her family and loves the sea.

From the Editor

Welcome.

Autumn is my favourite season, forever associated with new pencils, new school uniforms and frosts which turn the mundane magical. Many dread the coming of winter but I relish the shortening days and the falling temperatures. I love feeling cocooned in the dark.

Older people are sometimes described as being 'in the autumn of life', implying waning, declining, ebbing. This belies the vibrancy and potential of autumn. Autumn has a beauty as compelling as spring, even if our frosts are not as sharp nor as frequent as they used to be: rich colours, ripe fruit, brown furrowed fields newly sown, flooded water meadows shimmering as the sun sets in the late afternoon.

Pauline Matarasso's poem 'Autumn', which you can read on page 33, captures all this. Born in 1929, Pauline is writing and publishing into her 90s. Her poem ends with these darkly hopeful lines:

> *Darkly the chrysalis*
> *In armoured womb gestates*
> *Tomorrow.*

Autumn is a great season. In nature and in life, it has both challenges and joys. Even French existentialist, Albert Camus, agrees: 'Autumn is a second spring… when every leaf is a flower.' Autumn is to be embraced, not feared. It is a season of new beginnings, abundance and hope.

God bless you.

Using these reflections

Perhaps you have always had a special time each day for reading the Bible and praying. But now, as you grow older, you are finding it more difficult to keep to a regular pattern or find it harder to concentrate. Or, maybe you've never done this before. Whatever your situation, these Bible reflections aim to help you take a few moments to read God's Word and pray whenever you have time or feel that would be helpful.

When to read them

You might use these Bible reflections in the morning or last thing at night, but they work at any time of day. There are 40 reflections here, grouped around four themes, by four different writers. Each one includes some verses from the Bible, a reflection to help you in your own thinking about God, and a prayer suggestion. The reflections aren't dated, so it doesn't matter if you don't want to read every day. The Bible verses are printed, but you might prefer to follow them in your own Bible.

How to read them

- **Take time** to quieten yourself, becoming aware of God's presence, asking him to speak to you through the Bible and the reflection.

- **Read** the Bible verses and the reflection:
  - What do you especially like or find helpful in these verses?
  - What might God be saying to you through this reading?
  - Is there something to pray about or thank God for?

- **Pray.** Each reflection includes a prayer suggestion. You might like to pray for yourself or take the opportunity to think about and pray for others.

Breath of God

Erica Roberts

Although we are mostly unaware of the breaths we take, from our first to our last, our physical survival is dependent on the exchange of carbon dioxide for life-giving oxygen. Maya Angelou, the American poet and civil rights activist, speaks of the deep connection between our breath and fullness of life when she said, 'Life is not measured by the number of breaths we take, but by the moments that take our breath away.' As I have reflected on how God breathes his life into us – a breath that animates, sustains, inspires and restores – I have had my own breath taken away by the deep intimacy of God's life-giving breath.

Jesus said, 'I came that they may have life, and have it abundantly' (John 10:10, NRSV). We discover that living abundantly depends on receiving this gift of God's breath, a metaphor for the Holy Spirit, who was present at the beginning of time, breathing life into creation. The Spirit continues to fill us with new life in Jesus, so that we may be 'transformed into his image with ever-increasing glory, which comes from the Lord, who is the Spirit' (2 Corinthians 3:18, NIV).

Genesis 2:7 (NIV)

The first breath

Then the Lord God formed a man from the dust of the ground and breathed into his nostrils the breath of life, and the man became a living being.

The unadorned joy of hearing a baby's first breath represents not only our delight in the gift of new life, but also the anticipation of all that lies ahead. Each first breath reminds me of that wonderful refrain of praise in Psalm 139:14, 'I praise you because I am fearfully and wonderfully made; your works are wonderful.'

Our verse today paints a beautiful picture of how God crafted humanity. The Hebrew word for 'formed' is also used for a potter, who artistically shapes clay with their own hands. We see God here shaping us with his hands, a deeply personal portrayal of God skillfully creating us in his own image (Genesis 1:27). Of course, however, we are created from the dust of the ground, a reminder that it will be to the ground that our bodies return after we take our last breath.

Yet what unfolds next never ceases to take my breath away. We join the story in which God, who has just spoken the universe into existence, intimately comes face to face with his creation and breathes his own eternal life into humankind. This marks the beginning of our lifelong and life-transforming relationship with our creator God.

■ **PRAYER**
'Let everything that has breath praise the Lord. Praise the Lord'
(Psalm 150:6). Amen

Job 32:7–8 (NIV)

The breath of wisdom

I thought, 'Age should speak; advanced years should teach wisdom.' But it is the spirit in a person, the breath of the Almighty, that gives them understanding.

Most of us would like to be wise; but what is wisdom and how do we gain it? The ancient Greek philosopher, Aristotle, said that 'knowing yourself is the beginning of all wisdom'. Psychological study has shown that wisdom comes with age as values like empathy, resilience and humility develop throughout life, enabling a person to find resolution rather than fear in their later years. Despite the breadth of experience that comes with ageing, these studies also show that attributes of wisdom can be exhibited in our earlier years.

In Job 32, the young man Elihu bursts on to the scene. He has respectfully listened to Job's three older friends' unhelpful reflections about suffering and now, rather impetuously, demands a hearing. Whatever we think of Elihu, his passionate outburst in the following chapters provides a pause, preparing the way for God to eventually speak 'out of the storm' (Job 38:1). Elihu reminds Job of God's presence and purpose, even through suffering. In his own defence, Elihu declares that 'it is not only the old who are wise' (Job 32:9), but instead we should seek God's wisdom throughout all seasons of life. It is 'the breath of the Almighty' that will bring understanding and wisdom.

■ PRAYER

Almighty God, we pray for your understanding and wisdom in our older years. Amen

Job 33:4 (NIV)

God's breath brings life

The Spirit of God has made me; the breath of the Almighty gives me life.

As Elihu opens his passionate discourse in response to Job and his three critical friends (Job 33—37), he declares that his confidence to speak comes from being made by 'the Spirit of God' and his life from 'the breath of the Almighty'. Elihu then reminds Job of their humanity, of being made from clay, and thus Job need not be fearful of him.

For those who like statistics, I wonder if you know that we breathe in and out about 22,000 times each day. I'll leave you to calculate the number of breaths we take in a lifetime. Elihu declares that each breath we take comes from God. What an amazing gift and yet as I ponder this, what a responsibility too. With each breath we take, God is giving us life. Mostly we are blissfully unaware of this precious gift, until we become 'out of breath' ourselves. If we imagine God giving us each individual breath, I wonder if we can be confident like Elihu and boldly breathe out God's love, compassion and justice into a world that desperately needs to hear God's message of hope.

■ PRAYER

'Breathe on me, breath of God,
fill me with life anew,
that I may love the way you love,
and do what you would do.'

(Edwin Hatch, 1835–89)

Isaiah 40:7–8 (NIV)

The enduring breath of God

The grass withers and the flowers fall, because the breath of the Lord blows on them. Surely the people are grass. The grass withers and the flowers fall, but the word of our God endures forever.

I love the changing seasons, from new shoots pushing through the warming earth in spring, to the glorious splendour of a summer garden. Warm autumn colours follow, catching the low sunlight before nature hibernates for winter. Our world is fragile and fleeting, like the wayside grasses and flowers referred to by Isaiah as he catches the imagination of the Israelites in exile.

Isaiah reminds Israel that like nature, humanity is also fragile and fleeting. As the Israelites are exiled into Babylon, lonely, confused and fearful, Isaiah consoles them with words of hope and comfort. These words are for us too. Into our brokenness, our grief and our fear, Isaiah speaks of a God who is constant and never fails, a faithful God whose word really does endure forever. The Bible remains the most read book worldwide, with almost four billion copies sold in the last 50 years. The God who spoke hope into the lives of exiled Israelites continues to breathe hope into the lives of men and women across our world today.

■ PRAYER
Faithful God, thank you for the amazing truth that 'Jesus Christ is the same yesterday and today and forever' (Hebrews 13:8). May our world be transformed by your enduring word of hope and love. Amen

Ezekiel 37:4–5 (CEV)

Restored by God's breath

He then told me to say: 'Dry bones, listen to what the Lord is saying to you: "I, the Lord God, will put breath in you, and once again you will live."'

The imagery of this passage, made famous through the old spiritual, 'Dem Bones' by James Weldon Johnson, has become an anthem against racial injustice. In these words, from Ezekiel, African American slaves found a vision for a new future, where the oppressed were offered hope and restoration. Through Ezekiel, God spoke into the spiritual desert experienced by the Israelites while living in exile. We hear them cry: 'Our bones are dried up, and our hope is lost; we are cut off completely' (Ezekiel 37:11, NRSV).

Jesus said, 'I am come that they might have life, and that they might have it more abundantly' (John 10:10, KJV). In this passage in Ezekiel, God also promises Israel an abundant life, where they will be restored to their homeland (Ezekiel 37:12). However, like Israel, we must first receive the breath of God. Theologian Walter Brueggemann wonderfully describes the breath of God, as 'this unutterable, irresistible, undomesticated force that surges into history to liberate heal, remake, and transform'.* I wonder if we sometimes feel like those dry bones, thirsty for an abiding connection with God. Filled with God's life-giving and irresistible breath, each of us can receive God's healing, remaking and transformation.

■ **PRAYER**

Holy Spirit, breathe new life into my dry bones, so that I can live abundantly for you. Amen

*Walter Brueggemann, *Using God's Resources Wisely: Isaiah and urban possibility* (John Knox Press, 1993).

Psalm 39:5 (NIV)

A breath prayer

You have made my days a mere handbreadth; the span of my years is as nothing before you. Everyone is but a breath, even those who seem secure.

Psalm 39 is David's cry of lament as he wrestles with the cataclysmic consequences of his sin. He compares the span of his life to a handbreadth, one of the smallest units of measurement in ancient Israel, equivalent to a few inches. Compared to eternity, our lives are but a handbreadth. David was an accomplished leader, and yet in this psalm he recognises his limitations and the brevity of life: 'Everyone is but a breath.' The Hebrew word for 'breath' translates as 'vapour' or 'emptiness', like a child catching a soap bubble or our breath on a frosty day.

In his lament, David turns to prayer, seeking God's forgiveness and discipline. Pope Francis said, 'Prayer is the heartbeat of the church and our "Yes" to an encounter with God.' Despite his despair, as David pours out his heart before God, he recognises that 'my hope is in you' (Psalm 39:7). I wonder how we respond when life feels fragile. As David understood, prayer is the heartbeat of our relationship with our eternal Father, who is unconditionally present with us in our silence, our lament and our worship.

■ **PRAYER**

Pray the Jesus Prayer. Sit comfortably and become aware of your breathing. Repeat the following slowly:

(*Breathe in*) Lord Jesus Christ, Son of God,

(*Breathe out*) Have mercy on me. Amen

Luke 23:46 (NIV)

The breath of hope

Jesus called out with a loud voice, 'Father, into your hands I commit my spirit.' When he had said this, he breathed his last.

At the heart of our faith is the cross, where Jesus hung, alongside criminals and yet innocent. Jesus died as a young man, whose days were but a handsbreadth, and yet also as our Saviour, whose days are eternal. With God's life-giving breath illuminating scripture, it is poignant that the final moment of Jesus' life arrives as 'he breathed his last'.

In his book, *Being Mortal*, Atul Gawande speaks about helping 'people to end their stories on their own terms'. As I sat with my family, waiting for my father to take his final breath, we knew that his story was coming to an end peacefully after a well-lived life. We also knew, as C.S. Lewis writes in the final 'Chronicles of Narnia' instalment *The Last Battle*, that my father was entering a new story: 'Now at last they were beginning Chapter One of the Great Story which no one on earth has read: which goes on forever: in which every chapter is better than the one before.'

As Jesus breathed his last, he breathed out hope, ending this part of his story on his terms. Jesus died as our Saviour so we might have eternal life and begin Chapter One of the Great Story.

■ PRAYER
'For God so loved the world that he gave his one and only Son, that whoever believes in him shall not perish but have eternal life' (John 3:16). Amen

John 20:22 (NIV)

Jesus breathes on us

And with that he breathed on them and said, 'Receive the Holy Spirit.'

Can you imagine yourself in a locked room with the followers of Jesus? The disciples are confused and traumatised by the past days, and despite hearing that Jesus is alive, they don't fully understand. Then Jesus appears and breathes on them. The Greek word for 'breath', *pneuma*, like the Hebrew *ruach*, also means 'wind' or 'spirit'. Earlier in Jesus' ministry, speaking to the Pharisee Nicodemus, Jesus describes the Holy Spirit: 'The wind blows wherever it pleases. You hear its sound, but you cannot tell where it comes from or where it is going. So it is with everyone born of the Spirit' (John 3:8).

Although invisible, the consequences of the wind blowing are evident, from birds catching the breeze to wind turbines turning or a hurricane leaving devastation in its wake. The wind of the Spirit can also come quietly, blowing away our cobwebs, filling our sails or ruffling still waters, as he challenges us to turn afresh to God; or he may come in power, turning our lives upside down.

On this occasion, Jesus breathes peace into the disciples' confusion. The Holy Spirit knows exactly what we need, be it comfort, counsel or challenge. Whether the Spirit comes as a light breath or gale-force wind, he comes always to bring new life, encouraging us to share this gift with others.

■ PRAYER

Come, Holy Spirit, come; breathe on me today. Amen

2 Timothy 3:16–17 (NIV)

Breathing through scripture

All Scripture is God-breathed and is useful for teaching, rebuking, correcting and training in righteousness, so that the servant of God may be thoroughly equipped for every good work.

I love those times when God speaks personally through scripture. Whether words of comfort, wisdom or guidance, knowing that God is speaking directly into a situation is powerful; it is building faith and equipping us, as the second letter to Timothy says, for 'every good work'. It's also exciting when we discover unexpected connections in scripture or a new revelation, especially when we thought we really knew a passage inside out.

The Bible is like a treasure trove, full of gifts to sustain and inspire us. We never quite know what will emerge, but each gem offers a new perspective and the deeper we delve, the more we discover about our relationship with God. Pope John Paul II said: 'Let us take up this book!... Let us savour it deeply: it will make demands of us, but it will give us joy because it is sweet as honey.'* Psalm 19 reminds us that God's word is 'more precious than gold' and 'sweeter than honey'. Let's take time to savour God's word today as he continues to breathe out his truth through it.

■ **PRAYER**

Dear Lord, give me a new passion for your word as I delve deep into the treasure trove of scripture. Grant me grace for the challenges so I can discover the joy that lies within. Amen

*Ecclesia in Europa 65

Psalm 150:6 (NIV)

Breathing praise!

Let everything that has breath praise the Lord. Praise the Lord.

Psalm 150 is like the finale of a grand symphony. The composer has shared a story with us, the musicians have asked some questions, expressed their lament, offered moments of hope and then as the story is resolved, the music crescendos as we are swept up towards the finale. As in this psalm, the cymbals resound with those closing chords and the audience and orchestra are united in the delight of these moments of musical climax.

We have received the eternal gift of God's breath of life, wisdom and restoration, but how do we respond? In this short psalm, we discover that our unreserved response is to praise him, to praise him not just in church, but to take our praise into the rest of our lives, worshipping God in our homes, our communities and throughout creation. Charles Spurgeon, the 19th-century preacher, declared, 'Praise is the rehearsal of our eternal song.' Turning to praise, even when we feel far from God, even when life feels a struggle, is like the orchestra rehearsing for that final performance. Choosing to use our breath to praise God will revive our faith, giving us a glimpse of the eternal song that one day ourselves and all creation will join in with.

■ **PRAYER**

'To him who sits on the throne and to the Lamb be praise and honour and glory and power, forever and ever!' (Revelation 5:13).

Seasons of silence

John Rackley

As I get older, I find I have an ambivalent attitude towards silence. At times I really enjoy some 'peace and quiet', but there are also times of the day in an empty house when I wish I could speak to someone. I don't like empty silence.

As someone who has tinnitus, I am never in complete silence and so I have had to discover how to find a way which challenges the clamour of unwanted noise. It isn't easy.

One of the characters in E.M. Forster's novel *A Passage to India* speaks disparagingly of 'poor, little, talkative Christianity'. I know what she means. It is very rare on a Sunday morning to find a congregation just sitting quietly waiting for worship to begin. In my experience just before a service, all sorts of chitchat are bouncing off the walls. It can be very off-putting. Again, I don't find it easy.

I should also say that the Bible is a very talkative book – songs, arguments, stories, love poetry, political proclamations – there's hardly time to 'hear yourself think'. Silence just doesn't seem to have a place… Or does it?

1 Kings 19:12b (NRSV)

The silence in creation

And after the fire a sound of sheer silence.

I was climbing the side of Mount Sinai. The path was cut into a steep cliff, and I rested against the wall. Suddenly I realised I was quite alone. There was no wind and certainly no fire, but I was compelled to listen. What I could hear can only be described as 'sheer silence'. It was both unnerving and strangely comforting. I think it was an encounter with what the hymn 'Dear Lord and Father of mankind' describes as 'the silence of eternity'.

I know that heaven is meant to be full of choirs singing the praises of the Lord, but beyond all that and before God spoke the first words of creation, there is a profound absence of unnecessary noise.

All the struggles I have to find the right words and prayers; all the times when I feel my little croaky voice can't do justice to his glory; all that helplessness is in fact absorbed by the deep silence of our Saviour God. The silence of God is not indifference but a kind enfolding in his merciful grace. He immerses our tumbling thoughts and nervous chatter in an infinite embrace that enriches all that we are so that nothing needs to be said or heard. Wonderful.

■ PRAYER

Gracious God, when we are trying to say too much, still our racing thoughts and calm our agitated hearts with the blissful sound of your silence. Amen

Ecclesiastes 3:7b (NRSV)

The silence of patience

A time to keep silence, and a time to speak.

'Don't you tell me to shut up.' She was angry. She felt her views had been sidelined. The family were all having their say and one sister was trying to control the situation. Unfortunately she had not chosen her words wisely. The youngest had erupted in tearful rage and would not be silenced.

The visiting pastor tried his best but left the overheated household feeling he hadn't got very far. It wasn't that they were not listening to each other. There was plenty of that going on. They had heard each other's opinions too often and knew them back to front. What was missing was any willingness to pause and step back. No one was willing to be patient and hold their tongue – just for a while – however brief. If they had, maybe in their self-control and silence a new way would have emerged.

The Old Testament writer of Ecclesiastes states that everything has its season (3:1) and rightly places silence and talk together. Too often they are seen as opposites. The teacher declares both are important, and we need the God-given gift to know when each is appropriate.

■ PRAYER

Listening God, forgive me when I race to get what I want to say in before everyone else. Show me instead how to judge when my silence will speak volumes. Amen

Job 2:13 (NRSV)

The silence of the companion

They sat with him on the ground for seven days and seven nights, and no one spoke a word to him, for they saw that his suffering was very great.

'You are such a good listener,' I was told. Well, not always; but sometimes the intensity of what I was being told compelled me to hold my tongue.

Job's comforters don't usually get a good press and certainly not from Job, but when they initially sat with him, they were doing all that was necessary at the time. They were not in a rush. They got down to his level and felt what was happening to him.

Isn't it good when that happens? I hope you have experienced such empathy from a friend or family member. It gives us space. We can feel accepted. Not everyone we know can do it. Sometimes others can be embarrassed, or maybe what we are going through makes them feel powerless.

A hushed compassion, that leans into our distress without judging us or rushing to answers, will provide gentle support. It may need to endure for a long time. It is a sign of the love of God, who knows what we are made of and does not turn away.

■ **PRAYER**
Listening God, as Jesus sat among the people of his time and heard their need, may his Spirit help us to live in the same way and become a source of his compassion. Amen

Psalm 62:5 (NRSV)

The silence of prayerful patience

For God alone my soul waits in silence; for my hope is from him.

Jesus once criticised worshippers who spent all their time in long prayers because they thought it was a way of making God notice them. A friend of mine summed up this teaching by declaring, 'The closer you get to God, the less you have to shout.' I try to remember this when I'm tempted to sing even more noisily to demonstrate how earnest I am about my relationship with God.

The psalmist chooses another path. We are to turn down the volume, compose ourselves, just be in the presence of God and let him come to us in the way he chooses. We are saved by grace not by noise.

These days I am finding it harder to put my prayers into words. Maybe it's my age or that I get bored with myself. I don't want to babble on, and I feel that what I want to say just doesn't do justice to how I am. All I can offer is a tongue-tied trust. This psalm reassures me that God knows my thoughts even though I am not able to put them into words. He doesn't need carefully constructed sentences, just willing hearts and a faith directed towards him.

■ PRAYER

Lord, when it is too hard for me to find the words, may your Spirit receive my struggling silence and fill it with the gift of your mercy and help. Amen

Psalm 115:17 (NRSV)

The silence of oblivion

The dead do not praise the Lord, nor do any that go down into silence.

Recently I discovered a recording of my grandfather telling one of his stories. He died in 1963 and it was lovely to hear his voice again. It didn't bring him back, but his voice was strangely comforting. The silence of the dead is a chilling experience which the psalmist honestly faces. I'm afraid it burdens many people still.

Even for the most hopeful Christian, no longer hearing the voice of a loved one singing alongside us in a service can be a devastating experience. There is a horrid finality about death. Life is over. In fact, this is the view of death found in most of the Bible until we reach the New Testament.

Is it any wonder, then, that the resurrection of Jesus has brought so much joy? I love the line in the modern hymn that describes the risen Lord as clearing his throat and ending silence, for the good of us all.

This is how God deals with our experience of oblivion. There is more to come. He is the God who brings life out of death – isn't that why there is so much singing in heaven?

■ PRAYER

Loving God, you know there are times when I am really troubled by the thought of dying; support my faith in the risen Lord and help me trust you for my future. Amen

Isaiah 30:15 (NRSV)

The silence of saving faith

For thus says the Lord God, the Holy One of Israel: In returning and rest you shall be saved; in quietness and in trust shall be your strength.

I watched my little grandchildren in the park. They are never still. They scamper everywhere. They test every swing and climbing frame. Of course, when it's time to go they always want to have one more ride which goes on forever. I love their energy and try not to envy them too much.

Even they come to rest sometimes though, and it's just as delightful. We snuggle together to read a book, and from that peaceful moment rises conversation and questions and little comments on the events of the day.

God encourages us to discover the resources of composure. It is a time to ease up and stop the frantic desire for the next thing. It is taking time to really ponder the meaning of what we believe and letting it make a home in our hearts. It is not turning away from our responsibilities or becoming lazy; it is recognising the source of our strength.

God knows we are facing great changes in the future. It will come soon enough. We do not need to rush to meet it. Quiet, trusting preparation will do us far more good.

■ PRAYER

O God, when we get into a dither about things, help us to pause and trust you that little bit more. Amen

Isaiah 53:7 (NRSV)

The silence of courageous suffering

He was oppressed... and like a sheep that before its shearers is silent, so he did not open his mouth.

The prophet is describing the response of the servant of God to harsh tyranny. The words ring as true today as in the time of Israel's exile.

In Bangladesh I met street-people. We could not understand each other but their mute expressions spoke volumes. They were simply asking me to look, remember and respond.

As I get older, the more I want to speak my mind. I get frustrated at what I see as unjustified indifference towards hurting people. For others there is often a point when words have come to an end. A time comes when, like the sheep, we must face the inevitable, and there is a strange dignity in conceding that there is no way we can change what is going on. All we can do is offer an audacious silence.

In recent times people concerned about the climate emergency have glued themselves to roads. Delayed motorists have yelled abuse at them. Most of the protesters respond with silence. It has an eerie power. Of course, we have to speak up for justice, but I cannot forget the appearance of those people living on the streets of Dhaka. Their silence cried out for change, and I am still moved.

■ PRAYER

Almighty God, there is so much that is terribly wrong in our world; may I never become indifferent to the suffering of others. Amen

John 19:9 (NRSV)

The silence of trust

[Pilate] entered his headquarters again and asked Jesus, 'Where are you from?' But Jesus gave him no answer.

Pilate knew Jesus was different. He couldn't understand why so many people were against him, but Jesus wasn't helping by remaining silent. Yet there really was nothing else for Jesus to say or do. The evidence was plain to see. Pilate just had to do some clear thinking and make up his mind about Jesus. He had to take time to contemplate the silent Christ and let the answer arrive. But he was under pressure from vested interests, argumentative critics and insecure family members. He was being battered by everyone's opinion of Jesus. Pilate needed to make space for himself.

This is what the silence of Jesus was giving him. Pilate was asking the right question. He just needed the right amount of time to discover the answer. Jesus entrusted himself into the response of Pilate.

He always does. This is the remarkable nature of God. He does not dominate us. He takes us to the right question and then waits quietly for our reply. He is with us in our desire to know him. For some people this is a long journey but the trust of God in us never wavers. He simply asks us to look with uncluttered thoughts and meet his trust with our own.

■ **PRAYER**

Lord, help me not to be put off by your silence but let it become an invitation to look again at Jesus. Amen

John 12:24 (NRSV)

The silence of the falling seed

'Very truly, I tell you, unless a grain of wheat falls into the earth and dies, it remains just a single grain; but if it dies, it bears much fruit.'

As I write this, I am surrounded by the sounds of autumn. A local farmer is out tilling the soil, and seeds sown for next spring's crop are already coming through in some fields. A few weeks ago, the dog and I crossed one of those ploughed fields to find the seeds gradually sinking into the earth.

Have you ever heard the noise of a seed falling into the ground? No, neither have I. Yet their noiseless descent produces life and growth. Seeds are remarkable. They carry the future in them. They do not proclaim their presence. They become embedded in darkness and then come to the light of day in their own time.

I imagine like you, I hope to have sown some good seed in my life. I do not expect to see the full harvest. I simply trust that in the future, whatever I have sown may bear fruit – even the fruit of the Spirit.

'I've just been sowing some flowers for next year,' said my elderly neighbour, 'even though I may not be here to see them.' She wasn't, but I enjoy them for her.

■ PRAYER
Father, may I never despair that my life has not been worth it. Help me to trust you for its fruitfulness, whether I see it or not. Amen

Psalm 4:4 (KJV)

The silence in stillness

Commune with your own heart… and be still.

Finally, I return to the psalmist and to one of the first translations of the Bible into English. For over 400 years people have been reading these words as the pace of life has become faster and faster. Over those years, stillness is a gift that has become sadly neglected, yet it is an essential companion of silence.

I wonder if, like me, you wish that you could cope with silence more profitably, especially in prayer. Maybe the quality of being still can help us. One thing I have noticed about growing older is that I do like just to sit. I know it doesn't suit everyone and too much of it is unhealthy.

To simply sit still and not try to start a conversation with God, just accepting that I am in his presence, is like opening a door. Through that door come all sorts of feelings and ideas, memories, people and places. There might be the occasional word of scripture. As long as I don't try to shape the experience to my expectations, these things become my prayer.

Whatever this may achieve I have to leave up to God. He does move in a mysterious way even through my restlessness. All I can offer him is the desire to be silent and faithfully seek moments of stillness.

■ **PRAYER**

Lord, please calm me, enfold me in your eternal presence and let the blessing of silence come. Amen

The Gift of Years

 Debbie Thrower is the pioneer of BRF's Anna Chaplaincy for Older People ministry, offering spiritual care to older people, and is widely involved in training and advocacy. Visit **annachaplaincy.org. uk** to find out more.

Debbie writes…

Welcome!

When a child is born, everyone waits eagerly to hear what name the parents will give the baby. Whatever they choose will have a bearing on the child's sense of identity for life. My name, Deborah, has Hebrew origins and means 'bee'. In the Jewish scriptures – the Old Testament – Deborah was a prophetess and became known as a poet and judge. Sometimes I feel a bit like a busy bee; as a part of the Anna Chaplaincy team, we work hard to develop this way of offering spiritual care, love and friendship to older people across the country.

From a baby's first gasp, it is God's gift of breath that enables each of us to live. Breath as a metaphor for the divine gift of the Holy Spirit is explored in these pages. So too is the gift of silence – if we can stop being quite so busy occasionally, we might make room for God's 'still small voice' to get through. Another set of reflections considers the birds and bees of the natural world and what blessings they bring us. So, as you can see, it is a rich mix we set out for you in this edition. Enjoy!

Best wishes

Debbie

Meet Kate Powell

 Kate Powell is Alton's fourth Anna Chaplain, following in the footsteps of founder Debbie Thrower. Since September 2022 she has written a popular monthly column in the local paper called 'Growing old gracefully', focusing on some of the older people she meets in the course of her work and highlighting 'their amazing stories and fascinating lives'.

Kate grew up in a church-going family: 'I don't know if it was necessarily a Christian family,' she says, 'but it was certainly a church-going family. When I went to university to study English, I vowed I wasn't going to go to church, but oddly, God – not oddly at all – had other plans for me. Always, throughout my life, even while I was trying to escape him, he always put these Christian figures in my path, so I never fully escaped.'

It wasn't long before Kate met her future husband: 'It felt like all I wanted was for him to ask me to marry him. But when he did and we got engaged, it felt like something was missing and I quite quickly realised that if we didn't have God in our marriage, it wouldn't work.'

Living in London at the time, they went together to a Christianity Explored course. 'That's when I became properly Christian and when I started finding out more about the Bible and Jesus. Basically, we haven't looked back. It's been a very slow burning journey of service.'

When they moved to Winchester, they started getting involved in volunteering at church. Kate worked with different children's groups, before being asked to help lead the women's group on a Monday morning.

In her professional life, most of Kate's jobs were with older people, first with a housing association and then with Age Concern and now AgeUK.

These roles gave Kate 'a real heart for older people' which didn't fade after leaving work when her children were small.

When she did go back to work, it was to help her husband run his business, but because most of their clients were Americans she didn't have to start until 2.00 pm. Kate used her mornings to do voluntary work in the local prison and as a hospital chaplain on what used to be called the 'geriatric' ward: work she 'absolutely loved'.

When her husband sold his business, Kate knew that what she 'really wanted to do' was become a 'proper' employed chaplain. 'Even though I'd being doing the work as a volunteer and everyone was lovely and supportive,' she says, 'I did feel a little bit like I didn't have any backing behind me.'

Over lockdown, she signed up to do a year-long postgraduate training course in chaplaincy at Waverley Abbey College. After she qualified, she started to look for chaplaincy jobs. For a while nothing really came up until suddenly she discovered the Anna Chaplaincy job advert 24 hours before the deadline for applications.

'It was weird,' says Kate, but her varied career equipped her perfectly for the Anna Chaplain role. 'It all came together. There are five objectives with this job and all five different roles I've had met one of the objectives.'

One of those objectives was to raise the profile of Anna Chaplaincy in the wider community, and that's where the 'Growing old gracefully' series comes in, as Kate explains:

'I was always speaking to lots of older people as part of my job and I just thought these stories should be more widely known. I started asking a few of the older people if they'd be happy for me to try to tell their stories. I contacted the *Alton Herald* and they really liked the idea.

'It happened really quickly because there was one particular woman, Penny Carmichael, and she was really keen: she thought it was a brilliant idea. She wrote a lot of letters to the *Herald* and was quite well known around Alton. But she was dying and every time I went to see her, she asked me to pray that she would die quickly and peacefully.

'She wasn't frightened of death. She was so ready to die. We just had the most amazing conversation and I suddenly thought, gosh, you will die soon, and I said, before you die, you'll be my first "victim" for the series. She said yes, but you'd better hurry!

'So I came up with the title, "Growing old gracefully" and the five questions I now always ask, and went back to see her the next week. When the *Herald* printed the story, they called it "Penny makes her final contribution". Brilliant! Penny died two days after I did the interview.

'After she died, her son asked if instead of an obituary the interview could be published as her tribute: her own words were so beautiful.'

People are beginning to notice the stories and that's really encouraging for Kate and her team of Anna Friends:

'Older people are full of amazing stories and they're so inspiring. For me, the biggest reason for hope I've got is their resilience and their gratitude. I think generally, that's their attitude to life. They've endured hardship and they know they can come out the other side. Or they say, well, it's tough now, but I did enjoy all those years of it being easy. For me it's such a source of hope to know that suffering is part of life and rather than trying to escape it all the time, they seem to – not embrace it, that wouldn't be the right word – they experience it head on and then they're not frightened of it.'

A poem for autumn

 Pauline Matarasso was born in 1929 and has had a long and distinguished career as a translator and historian. In 2005 she published a collection of poems – 'The price of admission' – written over the course of 30 years. Catholic commentator Christina Odone wrote of the collection: 'These poems manage something altogether rare – to be at once transcendental and intimate.' We're grateful to Pauline for permission to include 'Autumn' here.

Autumn

Wasps cluster comatose
On the fermented fruit
Of brambles.
Death raids their paradise
Soft-footed. Lightened, the
branch trembles.

This is the dying time
When earth relinquishes
Its surplus,
Yielding it to the strong
Pull of the season's ebb
Without fuss.

Vanished all admirals
And painted ladies; soft,
No sorrow;
Darkly the chrysalis
In armoured womb gestates
Tomorrow.

Pauline Matarasso. Used by kind permission.

The story of Anna

 In *Sharing the Christmas Story*, BRF's 2022 Advent book, Sally Welch recounts the story of Anna, for whom Anna Chaplaincy to Older People is named. Simeon and Anna, both advanced in years, recognised the true identity of the infant Jesus when Mary and Joseph took him to the temple in Jerusalem to 'present him to the Lord', according to Jewish law. The reflection from Sally's book is called 'Signs'.

There was also a prophet, Anna, the daughter of Penuel, of the tribe of Asher. She was very old; she had lived with her husband seven years after her marriage, and then was a widow until she was eighty-four. She never left the temple but worshipped night and day, fasting and praying. Coming up to [Mary and Joseph] at that very moment, she gave thanks to God and spoke about the child to all who were looking forward to the redemption of Jerusalem.

Luke 2:36–38 (NIV)

In my pilgrim journeys I have had the privilege of walking alongside many different people, of all ages and backgrounds. One of the most interesting groups is comprised of those who have recently retired. Many of these are carrying out a promise made to themselves over many years – that they would celebrate the end of their period of full-time paid employment by making a significant journey. Others have only taken on board the idea of a pilgrimage in the few months preceding their retirement. And a few have set off on the spur of the moment, with little planning, simply heading out towards a distant destination.

Conversations with these fellow pilgrims have been interesting, surprising and occasionally very moving. Many walkers embrace the time for reflection, giving themselves space to look back over everywhere they have been and everything they have done and to give thanks for it.

Some are looking forward to the next stage of their lives, using the rhythm of walking as a background for thinking about their priorities and goals for the future. They have shared the experience and wisdom of years, as well as their hopes for the years ahead, and I have been the richer for it.

The story of Anna is one of wisdom and hope. There is always a danger of disregarding the contribution that those who are no longer in financially rewarding work can bring to society as a whole, and it is wonderful to read how Anna's faithfulness and prayer is rewarded by her glimpse of the Messiah. Her willingness to share her experience is also documented – she speaks about Jesus as one who will be instrumental in the 'redemption of Jerusalem'.

Anna has not stopped looking forward, and she has not ceased to live in hope. Her story honours her in its inclusion in the narration of Jesus' birth.

Each of us, whatever our age and abilities, can contribute to the well-being of society, not just in active ways, but, like Anna herself, by being a model of prayer and faithfulness. We can look to the future with hope, articulating our vision for a better world, enthusing and supporting others in their work as the body of Christ carries out God's work on earth.

As Paul writes to the church in Corinth:

On the contrary, the members of the body that seem to be weaker are indispensable, and those members of the body that we think less honourable we clothe with greater honour, and our less respectable members are treated with greater respect; whereas our more respectable members do not need this. But God has so arranged the body, giving the greater honour to the inferior member, that there may be no dissension within the body, but the members may have the same care for one another.

1 Corinthians 12:22–25 (NRSV)

Sharing the Christmas Story is available to buy at **brfonline.org.uk**

The birds and the bees

Derek Morgan

If you are like me, you will have read or heard the Genesis account of creation many times over the years. It was only recently, however, that I realised that God created birds on day five and all other winged creatures on day six. I can't help but wonder why he made birds on a separate day from bees. Why put bees and dragonflies in with elephants and lions? This is something that I'd like to ask our heavenly Father one day.

It got me thinking more about the birds and the bees, and I realised that we can actually learn an awful lot from them. Not just practical things like which birds lay which colour eggs or which bees make the best honey, but important biblical principles that show how we could and should be living our lives.

Over the next ten reflections, I hope to surprise you by uncovering some of the wonderful truths we can learn from ten of God's awesome little creatures, and I can almost guarantee that you will never look at these particular birds and bees in the same way again.

Please enjoy them and be blessed.

Colossians 2:6–7 (NLT)

The flamingo

And now, just as you accepted Christ Jesus as your Lord, you must continue to follow him. Let your roots grow down into him, and let your lives be built on him. Then your faith will grow strong in the truth you were taught, and you will overflow with thankfulness.

Did you know that the collective noun to describe a gathering of flamingos is a 'flamboyance'? What a great term for these pink-feathered creatures. When flamingos are born, they are a dull grey colour. Their elegant pinky-red colouring comes from the carotenoids in their diet of animal and plant plankton. Without this plankton they would remain an unattractive grey colour and could be overlooked as just another long-legged wader.

Flamingos only stand out because of what they take in, and this is the lesson for us. As Christians we should stand out by the way we behave, talk and act, and that is determined by what we take in. We need to be taking in the written word of God, listening to good scriptural teaching and, when possible, enjoying the fellowship of other believers. Then we will stand out as people who live life the way God always intended, and we will attract others to seek the kingdom too.

■ **PRAYER**

Heavenly Father, give us the desire to thirst after you, to want to learn more about you and to live a life that pleases you. For the sake of Jesus Christ our Lord. Amen

James 1:5–6 (NIV)

The bumblebee

If any of you lacks wisdom, you should ask God, who gives generously to all without finding fault, and it will be given to you. But when you ask, you must believe and not doubt, because the one who doubts is like a wave of the sea, blown and tossed by the wind.

Of the common species of bees, bumblebees are the largest in size. Their bulk gives them the ability to hold on to a flower, buzz their wings and literally shake it so it releases pollen. Several eminent naturalists have done aeronautical calculations and have determined that bumblebees should not be able to fly because of the weight of their large bulk, and yet they do. Here is a humanly impossible situation, yet God has a solution.

You may be in a difficult situation where you don't know which way to turn and there seems to be no solution. The good news is that God has a solution. Bring your situation to him, invite him to get involved, then look for a solution to become clear. If God can do the seemingly impossible for the humble bumblebee, he can do the seemingly impossible for you too.

■ **PRAYER**

Dear Lord, in Jeremiah your word says that you 'have plans for me' even when I don't see them. Please guide me in the way you want me to go and give me the faith to follow. Amen

1 Peter 5:8–9 (NLT)

The emperor penguin

Stay alert! Watch out for your great enemy, the devil. He prowls around like a roaring lion, looking for someone to devour. Stand firm against him, and be strong in your faith. Remember that your family of believers all over the world is going through the same kind of suffering you are.

The bird with the most unenviable of parenting tasks is the male emperor penguin. The female lays one egg, then the male must stand up all winter in freezing temperatures balancing this egg on his feet. Once hatched, a young chick sometimes wanders off and the risk is that another male penguin that has no chick will try to abduct it. The chick soon learns that the safest place to be is at the feet of his father.

The lesson that the penguin chick must learn can equally apply to us. In our Christian walk there is no safer place than being 'at the feet of the Father', so to speak. We are never safer than when we are spending time with him and walking in his ways. However, Satan, 'the father of lies', will try to drag us away. He will put temptation into our path to try to lead us astray. Don't let him.

■ **PRAYER**

'Our Father in heaven, hallowed be your name, your kingdom come, your will be done, on earth as it is in heaven… lead us not into temptation, but deliver us from the evil one' (Matthew 6:9–10, 13, NIV). Amen

Romans 12:2 (GNT)

The honeybee

Do not conform yourselves to the standards of this world, but let God transform you inwardly by a complete change of your mind. Then you will be able to know the will of God – what is good and is pleasing to him and is perfect.

Who doesn't like honey! Apparently, it's the only foodstuff that lasts forever and never spoils. Aside from their honey-making skills, honeybees have a sense of smell that is 50 times stronger than that of a dog. It may surprise you to discover that bees have been trained to detect bombs and can sniff out landmines three miles away. They can also recognise human faces, and bees kept in a hive can learn to recognise and build trust in their human caretakers.

The fact about bees getting to know their keeper echoes very much our own situation with regard to knowing God. The more time we spend in his presence, the more we will get to know him. Daily Bible reading, prayer and worship enable our knowledge of God to grow, and as we see answers to prayer we will build our faith and trust in him. Spending time with God brings peace, direction and joyful living.

■ PRAYER

Heavenly Father, increase my desire to spend time in your presence, that I may know you more and grow in my knowledge of your ways and your word. For Jesus' sake. Amen

James 1:5–6a (TLB)

The tinamou

If you want to know what God wants you to do, ask him, and he will gladly tell you, for he is always ready to give a bountiful supply of wisdom to all who ask him; he will not resent it. But when you ask him, be sure that you really expect him to tell you.

One of the most timid birds you will ever encounter is the tinamou. They look a bit like a partridge and scurry about on the ground. However, if they get disturbed, they panic and can fly straight up in the air at tremendous speed without looking where they are going. They've been known to fly straight into a tree and kill themselves or they come back down into water and drown. They often put themselves in more danger than the threat they were trying to escape.

What do you do when you find yourself having to make a fairly major decision? Are you like the tinamou and do the first thing that comes into your head? The best option is always to talk to God about it and ask him for wisdom and guidance. Think of the expression 'out of the frying pan into the fire': no one wants to get burned like that.

■ PRAYER

Gracious God, your word says that you always want the best for us and when we need guidance we can and should come to you. Help us never to forget this. Amen

Ephesians 4:29, 31–32 (NLT)

The teddy bear bee

Don't use foul or abusive language. Let everything you say be good and helpful, so that your words will be an encouragement to those who hear them… Get rid of all bitterness, rage, anger, harsh words, and slander, as well as all types of evil behaviour. Instead, be kind to each other, tenderhearted, forgiving one another, just as God through Christ has forgiven you.

If you'd never thought of bees as being cuddly, wait until you see a teddy bear bee. (They only live in Australia though.) These bees are fatter than most bees and they are covered all over in golden brown hair. Their legs are particularly hairy, and they have a remarkably long tongue, which can be as long as half the length of their whole body. It must be a challenge for them to keep that tongue under control.

Sometimes we humans also have a problem keeping our tongues under control. We find it so easy to say the wrong thing, utter an unkind word, give an angry retort or engage in slanderous talk. Secretly gossiping about someone behind their back may seem harmless but it can be so hurtful. We need to ask the Holy Spirit to fill us with the gentle Spirit of Jesus to help us to be wholesome with our words.

■ **PRAYER**

Heavenly Father, we so easily slip up and don't control our tongues as we should. Please help us to speak words that edify and encourage and are filled with love. Amen

1 John 5:14–15 (GNT)

The starling

We have courage in God's presence, because we are sure that he hears us if we ask him for anything that is according to his will. He hears us whenever we ask him; and since we know this is true, we know also that he gives us what we ask from him.

From a distance the common starling might look a rather boring black colour, but if you look more closely, its feathers are a variety of iridescent greens, purples and blues. Starlings make different sounds too and in particular, they can sing notes that are too high for us to hear. It's amazing to think that their communication is happening in a way that we don't have any awareness of.

We can think of prayer in a similar kind of way. The Bible says that when we pray God hears us, and that too happens in a way that we don't understand. Our minds can't grasp how thousands of people can all be praying at the same time, yet God hears each prayer as if it was the only one. Though we don't understand quite how it works, we must never doubt that God hears our prayers, even if he doesn't seem to respond to them. His timing is just different from ours.

■ **PRAYER**

Heavenly Father, increase our faith to believe that you always hear our prayers and that in your way and in your time, you will always give an answer. Amen

John 3:16–17 (NASB)

The mining bee

For God so loved the world, that he gave his only Son, so that everyone who believes in him will not perish, but have eternal life. For God did not send the Son into the world to judge the world, but so that the world might be saved through him.

Mining bees live in little tunnels in the ground and tend to be solitary rather than living in colonies. They vary greatly in size, with the smallest adults being only 2 mm long while the largest are up to nine times as big. The wonderful thing is that each species of bee is designed for a specific type of flower, and they are really good pollinators.

Just think about that smallest little bee: it may appear to be insignificant and easily overlooked by us, but God ensures it has everything it needs to thrive. If God cares for little creatures only 2 mm long, he is certainly not going to overlook you. You may feel insignificant or think you have nothing to contribute and are of no use to anyone, but God does not see you like that. To him, you are so important that he allowed his Son Jesus to die for you. You are of infinite worth to him.

■ PRAYER

Dear Lord, you are the great creator and you made me to be me. Thank you that you love me so much that Jesus died so I can have everlasting life with you. Amen

1 Samuel 16:7 (NIV)

The great northern loon

The Lord said to Samuel, 'Do not consider his appearance or his height, for I have rejected him. The Lord does not look at the things people look at. People look at the outward appearance, but the Lord looks at the heart.'

A waterfowl that is thought to be from the oldest bird species on the planet is the great northern loon. It's a pretty bird with interesting spotted/striped patterns on its body with a dark head and red eyes. Upon seeing one, you may be led to think, 'That looks so cute!' However, this bird is one of the most dangerous in the world. They have razor-sharp beaks and will target your head, neck and eyes.

It's a good reminder that you can't judge by outward appearance. When we see someone for the first time, we all make subjective judgements based on what we see – sometimes getting the totally wrong impression. What do people think of you and your character when they meet you? While they can see your face, only you and God know what your heart is like. We pray alongside David in Psalm 51:10, 'Create in me a pure heart, O God, and renew a steadfast spirit within me.' Don't have the vicious heart of the loon.

■ PRAYER
Dear Lord, the world will try to lead us down paths that we don't want to take. Give us the steadfast faith and strength of character to follow your ways. Amen

Ephesians 6:17–18 (NIV)

The worker bee

Take the helmet of salvation and the sword of the Spirit, which is the word of God. And pray in the Spirit on all occasions with all kinds of prayers and requests. With this in mind, be alert and always keep on praying for all the Lord's people.

The worker bee is a type of bee rather than a species of bee and they are found wherever bees live in a colony. Their name literally describes what they do from dawn to dusk, and they are key to the survival of the whole colony. The work they do changes as they grow through to maturity – starting as cleaners, then nursemaids, Queen's attendants, honeycomb builders, then finally collecting nectar and pollen. Their role within the colony changes but they never stop working.

This is a wonderful example of how we should be during our lifetime. God gives us different roles to fulfil throughout our lives and these will change over time. Many of us find we no longer have the stamina and energy for children's work, but there will always be things for us to do. Our infirmities need not limit our desire to witness and minister to people, nor must they reduce our prayer life. Prayer is key for the endurance of God's church.

■ **PRAYER**

Loving heavenly Father, throughout our lives you have called us to different forms of service. Show us ways we can continue to serve you through our prayer life, for Jesus' sake. Amen

Of greater worth

Clare O'Driscoll

Every morning my grandparents got down the wobbly cup and saucer I made in pottery class and filled it with a joyful pick 'n' mix of vitamins and pills, like beads in different shapes and colours.

They loved that cup and saucer. I remember feeling puzzled, thinking it wasn't really that good, a bit wonky and bumpy, with jagged half-moons where I had sunk small fingernails into the cold squidgy clay, and five-year-old thumbprints embedded, immortalised beneath the clear glaze. I found it hard to believe they thought it was so special, but for them it was a miniature treasure, a symbol of much more.

It's sometimes surprising where we find value, the unexpected things and people that become important to us. Sometimes we find it hard to believe that we are of worth too, both to God and to others. We can't always see what they see.

In the following reflections, we will ponder what God says about our worth, looking at how deeply we are loved by God, but also at how we choose to attribute value ourselves. Considering the gentle interweaving of all these things, we will see how God's valuing love is reflected in us.

Mark 9:7 (NIV)

Listen to him

Then a cloud appeared and covered them, and a voice came from the cloud: 'This is my Son, whom I love. Listen to him!'

I placed the dessert on the table, frowning slightly. My failsafe recipe had failed, and my poor guests ploughed politely through a bland stodgy pancake instead of the richly flavoured torte I'd been planning to wow them with.

We often look to our successes or failures to determine our worth and the world tends to collude with this. While my friends were kind about my failed pudding, society can set the bar rather higher before it offers us any kind of validation. Value can be a slippery thing, difficult to pin down and seemingly always changing, and the things we once relied on can fail us.

When I start questioning my worth on these terms, the last person I'm listening to is Jesus, but he has plenty to say on the subject. Subverting the norms by blessing the poor and downtrodden, his life, words and attitude echo what his Father God has told us throughout the scriptures: Come as you are; you are fearfully and wonderfully made; I love you; I will give my Son in exchange for your life. When we doubt our worth in life, the truth is found in Jesus' words. Listen to him.

■ **PRAYER**

Jesus, thank you that when I listen to you, you quieten the voices of the world. Amen

Matthew 10:31 (NIV)

Sparrows

'So don't be afraid; you are worth more than many sparrows.'

There was a phase of my life when everything felt too ordinary. Juggling work and my children's needs with no local family support and a frequent-flyer husband meant that, ironically, I felt both completely indispensable and wholly unimportant at the same time. There was no one to pick up the pieces if I dropped them, and yet I felt invisible. What did I have to offer the world? If ever I felt like one of life's 'sparrows', it was then.

It's no coincidence that Jesus chose to talk about what some might consider the lowest and least interesting of birds when making his point about our worth. He knew all about pecking orders. He understands there are times when we end up feeling like the human equivalent of sparrows. He sees social hierarchies, but then he turns them upside down: the last shall be first. Even sparrows have tremendous value; how much greater worth you have to God than sparrows.

As for my own 'sparrow days', it was only years later that I learnt how important they were, when people told me how much they had valued my presence back then. God uses our ordinariness and our normal daily lives coming alongside others to show his goodness to the world.

■ **PRAYER**

God of the ordinary and the extraordinary, when we feel small,
remind us of our deep value in you. Amen

Romans 8:28 (NIV)

Background value

And we know that in all things God works for the good of those who love him, who have been called according to his purpose.

Recently, I decided to have a go at screen-printing – something I'd always wanted to try. I planned out a neat travel poster-style print, with clean lines and tidy blocks of colour. 'Yes, but…' my art teacher ventured, 'how about making some abstract backgrounds and printing it on top?' It wasn't what I'd had in mind, but I trusted her judgement and decided to do a mixture – some on plain paper, others on wild abstract backgrounds. The results were fascinating. While the cleaner copies were neat and pleasing, the ones with messy backgrounds had more depth and drama, beauty even.

We sometimes wish our backgrounds were like clean pieces of paper, or perhaps that we could print over the mess and make it all neat and perfect. We forget that our background is part of us. It's part of what makes us who we are.

Rather like those clean sheets of paper, God redeems us and makes us new. Even the difficult, more abstract parts of us have value too. They are still part of us. That messy past, even the mistakes and pain, have shaped us into who we are today. Therein lies depth and beauty.

■ **PRAYER**

Thank you, Father, that you can use the messy parts of our lives and pasts to make us more fully human to others. Amen

1 Peter 1:7 (NIV)

Better than gold

These have come so that the proven genuineness of your faith – of greater worth than gold, which perishes even though refined by fire – may result in praise, glory and honour when Jesus Christ is revealed.

When I was 18, I moved alone to work in a Christian community in the south of France for six months. Despite being in a beautiful place that I loved, it was hard to leave behind everything I knew. Everything familiar had been stripped away. Without my cosy bubble of friends, I no longer knew quite who I was.

When you're first dropped into a foreign land, it is rather like going back to childhood. Ironically, this huge step of independence – moving countries – can make you feel more dependent and needy than ever, like a child sitting at the 'grown-ups' table. However, through the feelings of loss, I found layers of myself I'd never known before and maybe wouldn't have found without this 'refining'. I found myself relying on my faith in a new way, which I might not have found had I stayed in the security of my hometown.

When all the things I had thought so important were 'refined' away, I was left with the gold of my faith, properly recognising its true treasure, perhaps for the first time.

■ PRAYER
Gracious God, when it feels like we've lost everything we value in life, remind us that our faith in you is of greater worth than gold. Amen

Psalm 73:25 (NIV)

More!

Whom have I in heaven but you? And earth has nothing I desire besides you.

On the Sunday morning of our church weekend away, the leader split us into two teams, tipped a bag of plastic balls across the room and shouted, 'See how many you can get!' It's fair to say we all turned slightly feral, pushing past each other to grab as many as we could. Nobody cared about anyone else. We didn't even know why we were doing it, we just wanted to get as many as possible.

When the timer pinged and we counted the booty, she added casually, 'By the way, I didn't say "get the most".' Therefore, subverting our worldly understanding of value rather like Jesus did, the prize went to the team with the least.

It's easy to think the way to feel valued is to get more. Often, we don't even know why we're doing it; we just want to get as much as possible: wealth, achievements, possessions, even relationships. None of these are wrong, but the attitude of prioritising and relying on their abundance is damaging to our souls and affects how we behave towards others. Conversely, it is often in the releasing of such things that growth and wisdom come, where we learn to be more like Christ and where we find true value.

■ **PRAYER**

Thank you, Father, that nothing we can own or acquire will ever equal what we have in you. Amen

Matthew 6:20–21 (NIV, abridged)

Treasures in heaven

'But store up for yourselves treasures in heaven, where moths and vermin do not destroy... For where your treasure is, there your heart will be also.'

My heart sank as I read the best before date. We'd been saving the luxury biscuits for a special treat. Now they'd simply gone off. Admittedly this was just a minor, if annoying, lesson in the futility of stockpiling. However, when we make a habit of storing up 'treasures' in the hope of finding our worth there, we can miss out in far more significant ways.

When we focus on external things to bring us value – money, control or possessions – we risk judging ourselves by that same bar and losing sight of our deeper worth.

Conversely, when we treasure the things God treasures – justice, peace and care for others – we find ourselves at the heart of that treasure too. When we treasure what is of true value, we move ourselves closer to God's heart, a place where we are enfolded in love; a place which deepens our understanding of how precious we are to our maker.

Jesus doesn't tell us to store up our treasures in heaven simply because it is the right thing to do morally speaking, but because it is the very best thing for us, leading our hearts to heaven.

■ **PRAYER**

Loving God, teach me to cherish what is truly important and to always be in line with your heart. Amen

Philippians 4:8 (NIV)

In between storms

Whatever is true, whatever is noble, whatever is right, whatever is pure, whatever is lovely, whatever is admirable – if anything is excellent or praiseworthy – think about such things.

I gaze at the sharp clarity of sunlight in between stormy showers and the intensely vivid green the grass turns at that time. It is my favourite kind of light, bright rays contrasting with the indigo grey of the clouds.

Sometimes, on days like these, I hang my washing out despite past experience, and definitely against my better judgement. I can't resist. I know it will probably rain again, but somehow it still feels worth it. It's still worth trying even when we think what's ahead might be a little gloomy. Sometimes, fear of the future makes us lose sight of what we have, but there is value in the present, the moments of sunshine we have now and what God can do in our lives if we make the most of this time, if we 'hang the washing out despite our better judgement'.

Who knows, that rain might not even come. Even if it does, it doesn't alter the value of the sunshine we have now. If anything, it makes it all the more precious. Sometimes God gives us gifts in moment-sized packages: we have to accept them, grasp them and live fully within them.

■ **PRAYER**

Thank you, God, for the gift of the present moment. Help me always to look for the treasure within it. Amen

Exodus 33:19a (NIV)

Glory or goodness

And the Lord said, 'I will cause all my goodness to pass in front of you, and I will proclaim my name, the Lord, in your presence.'

At primary school, my friends and I had a tactic to ensure our work had its share of compliments. With no attempt to disguise it, we would openly negotiate: 'I'll say I like your drawing if you say you like mine.' In subtler ways, this kind of negotiation can continue into adulthood. We all long to be seen. Sometimes we look for glory for ourselves, for people to affirm the things we are good at. In this passage, however, when Moses asked to see God's glory, God showed him goodness. The glory was in the goodness.

Which one do we value most? When we look for glory, it is usually just because we want to be seen. God already sees us completely, and ironically, it's when we focus on his goodness, poured through us into the world, that we become more fully ourselves. While our achievements might impress others, it is our actual goodness, rather than what we're good at, that shows people who we really are. It is our goodness that feeds others with hope and shares God's healing on the hardest of days.

Where we want a bit of glory, God instead chooses to shine his goodness through us.

■ PRAYER

Thank you, God, that the value of goodness is always greater than the glory of achievement. Amen

Isaiah 45:3 (NIV)

Seeing the fruit

I will give you hidden treasures, riches stored in secret places, so that you may know that I am the Lord, the God of Israel, who summons you by name.

At the bottom of our garden we have several thick, clumpy raspberry bushes. When the season rolls around, I often wander down to pick the fruit. Sometimes it's easy, but other times there are slim pickings – just the odd half-ripe berry that refuses to budge from its bud. At first glance, the leafy mass seems pure green and void of fruit.

Then I take a closer look, pausing to scan the branches from all angles, and I realise there are whole bunches of plump berries I'd missed. Some are so obvious I can't believe I didn't see them. Others require a little more burrowing and are a challenge to reach, but are always worth the effort.

Sometimes we struggle to see where God is in a situation. Sometimes the gifts God has for us aren't obvious and feel a little hidden. Sometimes we study Bible passages we've read what feels like a thousand times before and it can feel like there's nothing new for us there. However, if we stay a while, looking from different perspectives and being prepared to dig a little, to reach deeper into the clumpy leaves of familiarity, God has fruit waiting there for us.

■ **PRAYER**

Father God, help us to stay with you and your word, pushing back the leaves to see the fruit. Amen

Philippians 2:5b–7a (NIV)

Contagious worth

Have the same mindset as Christ Jesus: who, being in very nature God, did not consider equality with God something to be used to his own advantage; rather, he made himself nothing by taking the very nature of a servant.

During his earthly life, Jesus went through more than his fair share of challenges and insults. Yet one thing he never had to question was his worth. He never needed to scrabble around looking to prove his value because he knew, deeply, who he was. He lived completely in God's love.

Sadly, there are some who abuse positions of power, constantly seeking to make others seem smaller than themselves. Jesus, however, simply wanted others to know how loved they were and, as such, treated them as higher than himself. Knowing his rightful place as the Son of God, he felt no need to shout about his own importance. From that place of power, he simply chose to love others in complete humility.

When we have even an inkling of how much we are worth to God, we too will simply want to pass it on. We no longer need to prove how important we are to others when we know just how important we are to God. Secure in that knowledge, our lives can reflect the deeply liberating value of God's love.

■ **PRAYER**

Father, may your cherishing love overflow in us as we follow your example to love and value others. Amen

Endings and beginnings

Therefore, if anyone is in Christ, the new creation has come: the old has gone, the new is here!

2 CORINTHIANS 5:17 (NIV)

This last quarter of the year is an interesting intersection of endings and beginnings. For many, September marks the start of a new school year, with all the challenges and opportunities that may bring. At the same time, we begin to see the end of the calendar year in sight. These beginnings and endings can be a useful time to reflect on the time past and the time to come.

For BRF's ministries, this time is a mixture of reflection and preparation. **Anna Chaplains** across the country are bringing fellowship and spiritual care to older people during this period where loneliness can be exacerbated. The **Living Faith** team are busy preparing resources to help people to explore their faith in the important seasons of Advent and, looking ahead, Lent. For **Messy Church**, this can be a busy quarter of the year, with many Messy Churches restarting after a summer break and planning ahead for the busy Christmas period. And our **Parenting for Faith** team are working to support parents and churches as many things change for children during this period.

While our work is constantly changing, we embrace the message of the Bible verse above – the old has gone, the new is here. We are excited for all the new ideas and projects we will be exploring in the months to come and we celebrate all that we have already accomplished in 2023. Our vital work would not be possible without kind donations from individuals, charitable trusts and gifts in wills. If you would like to support BRF's work now and in the future you can become a Friend of BRF by making a monthly gift of £2 a month or more – we thank you for your friendship.

Find out more at **brf.org.uk/donate** or get in touch with us on **01235 462305** or via **giving@brf.org.uk**.

Judith Moore
Fundraising development officer

This book engages with two great Christmas hymns: the Magnificat and Benedictus. It is also rooted in poets, prophets and the theology and devotional writing of the black theologian and mentor to Martin Luther King Jr., Howard Thurman. Using the *lectio divina* approach to passages drawn from Isaiah and Luke, *An Advent Manifesto* is an invitation to pray and practise that most ancient Advent prayer, 'Come, Lord Jesus, come.'

An Advent Manifesto
Daily readings and reflections from Isaiah and Luke
Martyn Percy
978 1 80039 094 2 £9.99
brfonline.org.uk

In 25 short reflective pieces written by Claire Musters, we travel through promise and preparation to joy, peace and finally love. Along the way we encounter a choir of 40 diverse voices sharing their favourite carols, hymns, poems and prayers, illustrated throughout with original colour artwork. This Christmas, let us take the time to slow down, reflect and thank God for all the ways he is at work in our lives each day.

Christmas Voices
Reflections, carols, poems and prayers for the festive season
Claire Musters
978 1 80039 230 4 £9.99
brfonline.org.uk

To order

Online: brfonline.org.uk
Telephone: +44 (0)1865 319700
Mon–Fri 9.30–17.00
Post: complete this form and send to the address below

Delivery times within the UK are normally 15 working days. Prices are correct at the time of going to press but may change without prior notice.

Title	Issue	Price	Qty	Total
An Advent Manifesto		£9.99		
Christmas Voices		£9.99		
Sharing the Christmas Story		£8.99		
Bible Reflections for Older People (single copy)	Sep–Dec 2023	£5.50		
Bible Reflections for Older People (single copy)	Jan–Apr 2024	£5.50		

POSTAGE AND PACKING CHARGES			
Order value	UK	Europe	Rest of world
Under £7.00	£2.00		
£7.00–£29.99	£3.00	Available on request	Available on request
£30.00 and over	FREE		

Total value of books	
Donation	
Postage and packing	
Total for this order	

Please complete in BLOCK CAPITALS

Title .... First name/initials .... Surname..

Address ....

.... Postcode ....

Acc. No. .... Telephone ....

Email ....

Method of payment

❏ Cheque (made payable to BRF)   ❏ MasterCard / Visa

Card no. ☐☐☐☐ ☐☐☐☐ ☐☐☐☐ ☐☐☐☐

Expires end ☐☐ ☐☐   Security code ☐☐☐   Last 3 digits on the reverse of the card

We will use your personal data to process this order. From time to time we may send you information about the work of BRF. Please contact us if you wish to discuss your mailing preferences **brf.org.uk/privacy**

Registered with FUNDRAISING REGULATOR

Please return this form to:

BRF, 15 The Chambers, Vineyard, Abingdon OX14 3FE | **enquiries@brf.org.uk**
For terms and cancellation information, please visit brfonline.org.uk/terms.

Bible Reading Fellowship (BRF) is a charity (233280) and company limited by guarantee (301324), registered in England and Wales

BIBLE REFLECTIONS FOR OLDER PEOPLE **GROUP SUBSCRIPTION FORM**

All our Bible reading notes can be ordered online
by visiting **brfonline.org.uk/subscriptions**

The group subscription rate for *Bible Reflections for Older People* will be £16.50 per person until April 2024.

☐ I would like to take out a group subscription for .... (*quantity*) copies.

☐ Please start my order with the January 2024 / May 2024 / September 2024* issue.
(*delete as appropriate*)

Please do not send any money with your order. Send your order to BRF and we will send you an invoice.

Name and address of the person organising the group subscription:

Title .... First name/initials .... Surname...

Address..

.... Postcode ....

Telephone .... Email..

Church..

Name and address of the person paying the invoice if the invoice needs to be sent directly to them:

Title .... First name/initials .... Surname...

Address..

.... Postcode ....

Telephone .... Email..

Please return this form to:
BRF, 15 The Chambers, Vineyard, Abingdon OX14 3FE | **enquiries@brf.org.uk**
For terms and cancellation information, please visit brfonline.org.uk/terms.

Bible Reading Fellowship is a charity (233280) and company limited by guarantee (301324), registered in England and Wales

BROP0323

BIBLE REFLECTIONS FOR OLDER PEOPLE **INDIVIDUAL/GIFT SUBSCRIPTION FORM**

> To order online, please visit **brfonline.org.uk/subscriptions**

☐ I would like to take out a subscription (*complete your name and address details only once*)
☐ I would like to give a gift subscription (*please provide both names and addresses*)

Title .... First name/initials .... Surname ....

Address ....

.... Postcode ....

Telephone .... Email ....

Gift subscription name ....

Gift subscription address ....

.... Postcode ....

Gift message (*20 words max. or include your own gift card*):

....

....

Please send *Bible Reflections for Older People* beginning with the January 2024 / May 2024 / September 2024* issue (*delete as appropriate*):

(*please tick box*)	UK	Europe	Rest of world
Bible Reflections for Older People	☐ £20.85	☐ £28.05	☐ £32.10

Total enclosed £ .... (*cheques should be made payable to 'BRF'*)

Please charge my MasterCard / Visa with £ ....

Card no. ☐☐☐ ☐☐☐☐ ☐☐☐☐ ☐☐☐

Expires end ☐☐ ☐☐ Security code ☐☐ Last 3 digits on the reverse of the card

We will use your personal data to process this order. From time to time we may send you information about the work of BRF. Please contact us if you wish to discuss your mailing preferences **brf.org.uk/privacy**

Please return this form to:
BRF, 15 The Chambers, Vineyard, Abingdon OX14 3FE | **enquiries@brf.org.uk**
For terms and cancellation information, please visit brfonline.org.uk/terms.

BRF

Bible Reading Fellowship is a charity (233280) and company limited by guarantee (301324), registered in England and Wales